Hanson, Anders

What in the world

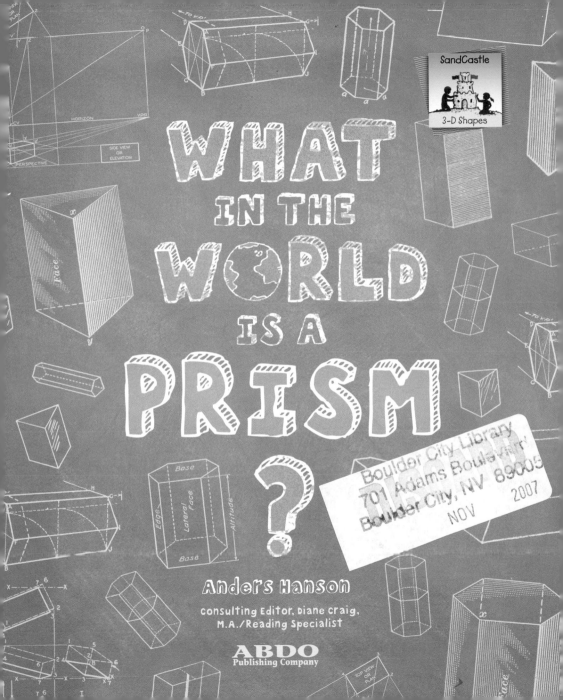

Published by ABDO Publishing Company, 8000 West 78th Street, Edina, MN 55439.

Copyright © 2008 by Abdo Consulting Group, Inc. International copyrights reserved in all countries.

No part of this book may be reproduced in any form without written permission from the publisher. SandCastle™ is a trademark and logo of ABDO Publishing Company.

Printed in the United States.
Editor: Pam Price
Curriculum Coordinator: Nancy Tuminelly
Cover and Interior Design and Production: Mighty Media
Photo Credits: BananaStock Ltd., JupiterImages Corporation, ShutterStock

Library of Congress Cataloging-in-Publication Data

Hanson, Anders, 1980-
  What in the world is a prism? / Anders Hanson.
    p. cm. -- (3-D shapes)
  ISBN 978-1-59928-889-5
  1. Prisms--Juvenile literature. 2. Shapes--Juvenile literature. 3. Geometry, Solid--Juvenile literature.
  I. Title.
  QA491.H366 2008
  516'.156--dc22

                        2007010193

SandCastle™ Level: Transitional

Emerging Readers
(no flags)

Beginning Readers
(1 flag)

Transitional Readers
(2 flags)

Fluent Readers
(3 flags)

SandCastle™ would like to hear from you. Please send us your comments or questions.

sandcastle@abdopublishing.com

3-D shapes are all around us.

3-D stands for 3-dimensional.

It means that an object is not flat.

A prism is a 3-D shape.

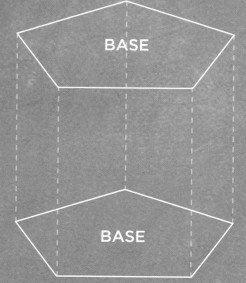

BASE

BASE

The bases of a prism are identical, parallel polygons.

The bases are connected by parallelograms.

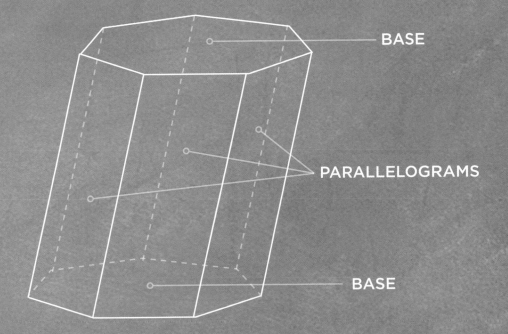

BASE

PARALLELOGRAMS

BASE

The number of parallelograms is equal to the number of sides of the bases.

Prisms are everywhere!

Sarah drinks from a juice box.

The juice box is a rectangular prism.

Rectangular prisms have four sides.

Triangular prisms
can make rainbows!

Have you ever
made a rainbow?

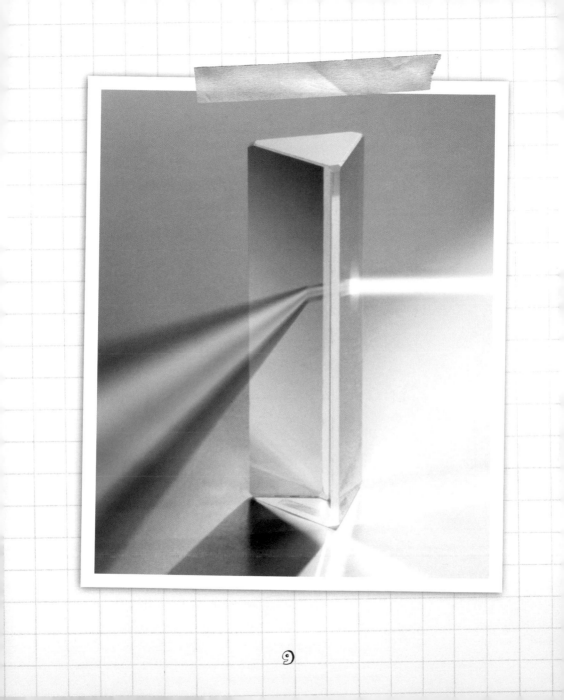

A prism can have
many sides.

Most of the boxes
in this picture have
either six or eight
sides.

These blocks
are cubes.

A cube is a
kind of prism.

Jennifer's family
is moving in to a
new house.

The moving boxes
are prism shaped.

Sandy makes a phone
call from inside an
old phone booth.

The phone booth is
shaped like a prism.

Many skyscrapers
are prism shaped.

Have you ever seen
a skyscraper?

Find the prisms!

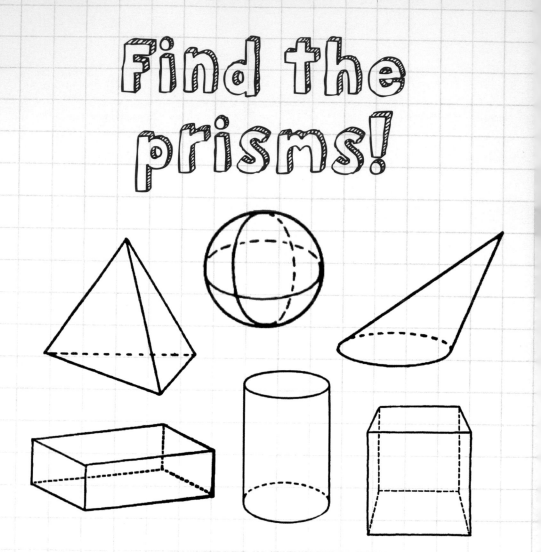

Which two of these 3-D shapes are prisms?
Remember, a cube is a kind of prism!

How many prisms can you find in this photo?

21

Everyday prisms

Take a look around you.

Do you see any prisms?

How to draw a prism

1. Draw a rectangle.

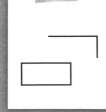

2. Draw a right angle next to the rectangle.

3. Connect the right angle and the rectangle with three straight lines.

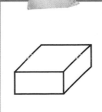

Glossary

dimensional – having a measurement of length, width, or thickness.

identical – exactly the same.

parallel – the state in which two lines or shapes are an equal distance apart. Parallel lines or shapes do not meet.

parallelogram – a four-sided shape in which the opposite sides are parallel.

polygon – a two-dimensional shape with any number of sides and angles.

right angle – an angle that measures 90 degrees.

To see a complete list of SandCastle™ books and other nonfiction titles from ABDO Publishing Company, visit www.abdopublishing.com.
8000 West 78th Street, Edina, MN 55439 · 800-800-1312 · 952-831-1632 fax